My

Relationship

is

Over

Written By:

Dee Henderson

Copyright Notice

Who am I?

How do I see myself?

How do I feel about myself?

How do my friends/loved ones see me?

What is my age now?

How much relationship experience do I have?

In this book, you will examine your feelings, responses, and behaviors, so that you may identify what went wrong in past relationships, and hopefully find the strength in yourself to be able to change enough to have good future relationships.

My ex-partner's name is:

What words describe my ex-partner? Check as many or as few as applied during any stage of our relationship:

[ ] attentive	[ ] kind	[ ] loving
[ ] demanding	[ ] attractive	[ ] fun
[ ] intense	[ ] emotional	[ ] funny
[ ] affectionate	[ ] smart	[ ] shy
[ ] forceful	[ ] friendly	[ ] clean
[ ] aggressive	[ ] passive	[ ] moody
[ ] emotionless	[ ] immature	[ ] sexual
[ ] passionate	[ ] detached	[ ] loud
[ ] independent	[ ] dependent	[ ] quiet
[ ] outgoing	[ ] distant	[ ] sweet
[ ] thoughtful	[ ] selfish	[ ] giving
[ ] _____	[ ] _____	[ ] _____

What did I like the best?

What bothered me the most?

Was my ex-partner good at communication?
[ ] Yes   [ ] No   [ ] Sometimes

Was my ex-partner emotionally open with me?
[ ] Yes   [ ] No   [ ] Sometimes

Did I ever feel uncomfortable around my ex-partner?   [ ] Yes   [ ] No
If yes, why?

Do I feel that I 'lost' my ex-partner, that I 'chased away' my ex-partner, or something else (escaped? outgrew? etc.)?

How We Met

Sometimes, when we look back at things, we discover that the first contact we had with someone should have given us an insight into the future we might share with them. Of course, we are all less than perfect, and we do not always pay close attention to details that should give us clues, or to our instincts. It is also true that we sometimes ignore our instincts. This can be because of the thrill of newness, or because we habitually delude ourselves, or because of any number of other reasons.

When did we meet?

Where did we meet?

Did we have any connection? (Friends in common, occupational connections, etc.) [ ] Yes [ ] No   [ ] Not that we knew of at the time

What were my first impressions of my ex-partner?

What is 'our story' of how we became a couple?

First Days

When a relationship is new, it is often thought of as the best time in the relationship. It is generally full of romance, the intensity of newness, and all that comes with falling in love. It is fun and we often see things through 'rose-colored glasses' and do not pay full attention to things that we would otherwise notice. Sometimes during this time, we notice little things that we find 'cute' or only slightly annoying; things that later become intolerable to us.

What were some of the things I noticed, but tolerated in the beginning, that I could not tolerate later on in the relationship?

What did I think of these things at the time?

What fun things did we do in the beginning, that we stopped doing later on?

Why did we stop doing these things?

Was this the best time in our relationship?
[ ] Yes   [ ] No
Why or why not?

Did we make plans for a future together?
[ ] Yes   [ ] No
If yes, what did we plan, and did I believe that we both wanted those plans to happen?

Did everything seem 'good', or did it seem 'too good to be true'? Explain.

The First Big Change

At times in our lives, we become aware of things that are happening around us, but we don't want them to be true, so we tell ourselves that nothing is happening. This denial is damaging to us, but we still do it. It is also true that some things happen that we simply do not notice. This is generally because we are afraid that those things will happen, so we keep ourselves blind to those events. This is damaging, but our fear can sometimes override our common sense.

Did I notice something had changed?
[ ] Yes   [ ] No
If yes, did I know what had changed, or did I just know that something was now different? Explain.

What was the change?

What caused it? (if I know)

What was my reaction to the change?

Could I have prevented this change?
[ ] Yes   [ ] No
If yes, how? If no, why not?

How did I feel about the change?

What was my ex-partner's reaction to the change?

How do I think my ex-partner felt about it?

Where it All Went Wrong

Often, we can reverse things if we address them early enough, but as humans, we tend to ignore them instead. When the issue becomes too big to ignore, we then try to 'fix' them, only to find that it is too late. At this point, we should turn our attention and reflection inward, to see where WE can adapt and make things right, but too often we begin to accuse our partner of not doing all that can be done to make it right. Making accusations without trying to calmly talk issues through can actually turn something that might be salvaged into something that nothing can save.

Was there a big event that caused the relationship to turn bad?   [ ] Yes   [ ] No
If yes, what was it? If no, what happened over time to make it go wrong?

Did I do anything to try to stop it?
[ ] Yes   [ ] No
If yes, what did I do? If not, why not?

Did I do things that helped it to go wrong?
[ ] Yes   [ ] No
If yes, what did I do?

Did my ex-partner do anything to try to stop it?
[ ] Yes   [ ] No
If yes, what did my ex-partner do? If not, why
do I think that?

At that point, was there anything that could
have stopped it from turning all wrong?
[ ] Yes   [ ] No
If yes, what might have changed it? If not, why
not?

The Final Days

During the final days, when you are still a couple, but can see the end looming near, the best thing you can do is stay calm, speak gently, and offer encouragement. Even if your heart is breaking and you feel overwhelmed by it all, and no matter how hard it might be, you should do your very best to not make it any harder for either of you. It is understandable that you may want to strike out in anger, hurt, or resentment, but clear your mind, and try to see beyond, to the greater picture. Use this time for silent self-reflection, or to think ahead to your own future. Yelling, screaming, crying, and breaking down will do you no good. If you are truly in your final days of the relationship, none of these things will help either of you. Also, they will not make you feel any better.

Toward the end of the relationship, was there a silence between us that wasn't there before?
[ ] Yes   [ ] No
If yes, who initiated the silence?

Was there arguing or fighting? [ ] Yes   [ ] No
If yes, what was it about?

Honestly, who initiated the arguing or fighting?

Do I feel that I responded appropriately to the stressors of our final days?   [ ] Yes   [ ] No
If yes, why? If no, why not?

Do I feel that my ex-partner responded appropriately to those same stressors?
[ ] Yes   [ ] No   If yes, why? If no, why not?

Did I behave appropriately?   [ ] Yes   [ ] No
If no, why not? How did I behave?

Did my ex-partner behave appropriately?
[ ] Yes   [ ] No   If no, why not?
How did my ex-partner behave?

What was I feeling during this time?

What do I think my ex-partner was feeling during this time?

Did I give my ex-partner a chance to talk about us during this time? [ ] Yes   [ ] No
If yes, did my ex-partner try to talk to me?
[ ] Yes   [ ] No
If yes, what did my ex-partner say?

How did I respond or behave?

Was this an appropriate response or behavior?
[ ] Yes   [ ] No   How do I feel now about it?

Did my ex-partner give me a chance to talk about us during this time? [ ] Yes   [ ] No
If yes, did I take the opportunity to try to talk to my ex-partner? [ ] Yes   [ ] No

If yes, what did I say?

If no, why didn't I talk?

How did my ex-partner respond or behave?

Was this an appropriate response or behavior?
[ ] Yes   [ ] No   How do I feel about it?

As humans, we cannot stop ourselves from feeling, but we can control our behavior and most of our responses to those feelings. While it's true that some people do not have adequate control over their emotions, we all DO have control over our physical and verbal responses and behavior. For example, no matter how hurt or angry we are, we can control whether or not we throw things, scream and yell, or become abusive. Choosing our responses and behaviors appropriately can dictate what kind of, if any, ongoing relationship we have with our ex-partner. If you have children, you WILL have an ongoing relationship with that person, and it will be vital that you can at the very least be civil to one another.

The Split

Sometimes we linger in a relationship, even after we know it's over, until something causes us to finally make the break. This act of separating can be just as hard as knowing it's over. Old feelings, both good and bad, can come to the surface again, and cause new hurts.

What was the date when we 'officially' were no longer a couple?

Was there something that happened that caused the actual split to happen on this day?
[ ] Yes   [ ] No   If yes, what happened?

How did I feel about it at the time?

How do I feel about it now?

The way I see it, the fault for this breakup lies with [ ] Me.   [ ] My ex-partner.   Why?

Do I feel that I did everything I could to keep the relationship together?   [ ] Yes   [ ] No
If yes, what things did I do? If no, why not?

Why do I think each of these things was not effective?

Did my ex-partner do everything possible to keep us together?   [ ] Yes   [ ] No
If yes, what things did my ex-partner do? If no, why not?

Why do I think each of these things was not effective?

How do I feel about all these things now?

Separate Lives

After a breakup, we both must find new lives, separate from one another. It can be hard, especially for the person who feels that they were 'left behind' by the other person. We must let the other person go on with a new life, without our interference, as we go on with ours.

After we separated, where did I go? Why?

Where did my ex-partner go? Why?

What is my life like now? Why is it like this?

Do I know anything about my ex-partner's new life? If so, what do I know? Why do I know this?

Can I let go, and let my ex-partner have a new life, completely separate from mine?
[ ] Yes   [ ] Yes, with hesitation   [ ] No
Explain.

What has happened with 'our' friends? How do I feel about it?

Do I feel that I had to give up some things that I shouldn't have had to give up?
[ ] Yes   [ ] No   If yes, what things, and why do I feel I shouldn't have had to give them up?

Am I ready to face life without my ex-partner?
[ ] Yes   [ ] No
If yes, why? If no, why not?

Moving On

Moving on can bring feelings of relief, hope, and peace. It is a big life change, and sometimes it can be frightening to face, but this is one change we should embrace. Moving on is healthy, and should bring us feelings that reflect that.

Did I give the relationship my all?
[ ] Yes   [ ] No   If yes, why? If no, why not?

Can I be proud of my words, actions, and responses during the relationship?
[ ] Yes   [ ] No   If yes, why? If no, why not?

Can I be proud of my words, actions, and responses during the breakup?
[ ] Yes   [ ] No   If yes, why? If no, why not?

Am I afraid to move on?   [ ] Yes   [ ] No
If yes, why? If no, why not?

Do I feel ready to move on?   [ ] Yes   [ ] No
If yes, why? If no, why not?

Do I feel like I'll ever be able to love again?
[ ] Yes   [ ] No   If yes, why? If no, why not?

Do I feel like I will ever be loved again?
[ ] Yes   [ ] No   If yes, why? If no, why not?

Why It's OK Now To Be Apart

Life is full of changes. Many of those changes turn out to be good for us, even if we can't see it when we're going through them. We want to not only survive life's changes, but to emerge on the other side of them as a better, stronger, wiser person. Sometimes we feel that we aren't strong enough to survive changes that come our way, but we truly are strong enough. There is nothing we can't overcome, although sometimes we have to ask for help, which takes a strength of its own, rather than a weakness. One thing to remember is that a burden shared is only half a burden...

The end of a relationship is a major life change. It hurts, but you <u>will</u> get through it, and good things will happen to you again.

Do you believe that everything is going to be OK for you without this relationship?

[ ] Yes   [ ] No   If yes, why? If no, why not?

Do you have people you can talk to, or lean on, during times when it all seems to be too much to bear?   [ ] Yes   [ ] No
If no, why not? If yes, who are the people in your support system?

What do these people tell you that gives you hope and encouragement for the future?

My Short-Term Goals   (For the next year)

My Future Goals (One to Five Years)

My Long-Term Goals (5+ Years)

Loving Me For Me

Ways I can show my love for myself:

Things I want to do, just for me:

Ways I can show appreciation for myself:

Gifts I want to give myself to remind me that I am deserving of love and happiness:

Happiness For My Future

My new Hopes and Dreams:

Things that make me happy now:

Reasons to smile every day:

The New, Improved Me!

A description or drawing of myself, ready to face the future:

Other Thoughts

Other Feelings

Old Photos From the Relationship

Old Photos From the Relationship

My Goodbye Letter to the Relationship

(Letter, continued...)

www.ingramcontent.com/pod-product-compliance
Lightning Source LLC
Chambersburg PA
CBHW061936280526
45787CB00004B/1619